Piano • Vocal • Guitar

Top Hits of 1997

ISBN 0-7935-8708-5

7777 W. BLUEMOUND RD. P.O. BOX 13819 MILWAUKEE, WI 53213

Visit Hal Leonard Online at
www.halleonard.com

Piano • Vocal • Guitar

Top Hits of 1997

CONTENTS

ALL BY MYSELF

Music by SERGEI RACHMANINOFF
Words and Additional Music by ERIC CARMEN

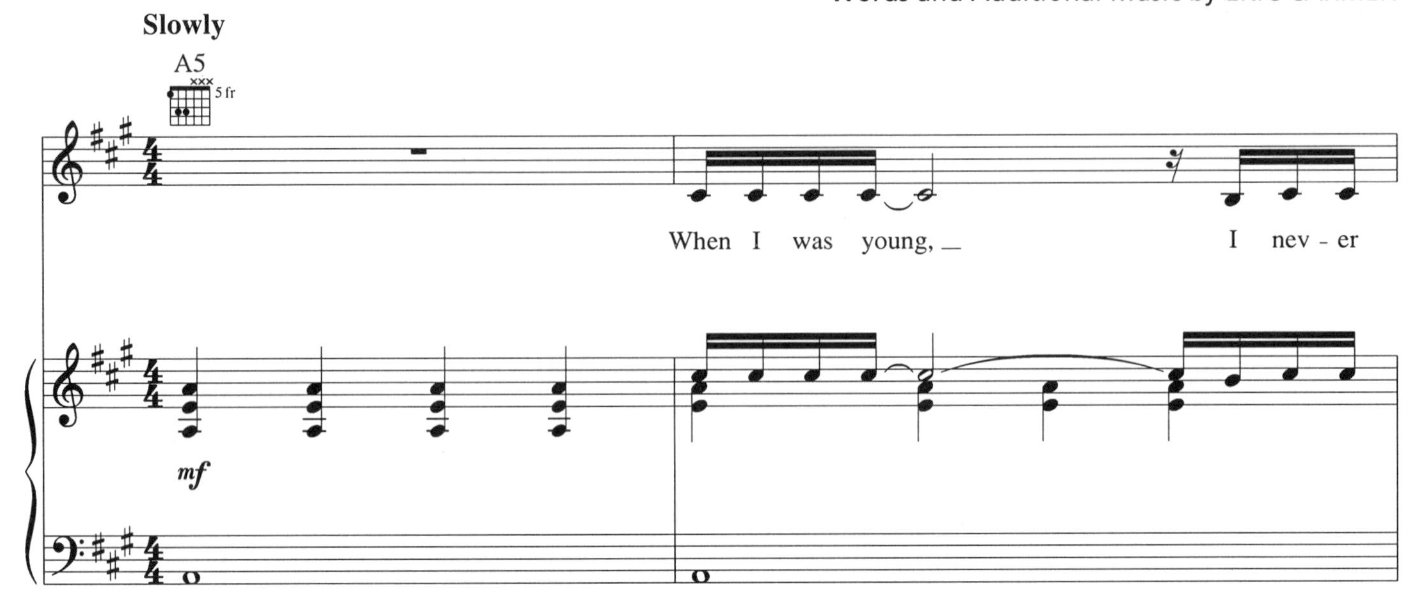

A
Dm6/A
A
Liv-in' a-lone,
I think of all the friends I've known.
Hard to be sure.
Some-times I feel so in-se-cure,
a tempo
Em6/G
F#7sus
F#7
Bm
Dm
But when I dial the tel-e-phone,
no-bod-y's home.
and loves so dis-tant and ob-scure
re-mains the cure.
A/C#
A7
F#
F#7
B7
Dm/F
E7sus
E7
A
All by my-self,
poco rit.
a tempo
C#m7
4fr
G6
F#7sus
F#7
1
Bm
Bdim/F
E7
don't wan-na be all by my-self any-more.

Bm
Bdim/F
E7
A
C♯m7
4fr
self an - y - more.
All by my - self,
don't wan-na live
G6
F♯7sus
F♯7
Bm
Dm
C♯
all by my - self any - more.
Freely, moderately
Cmaj7
B
Em
D/F♯
G
Am
F♯m7♭5
B7sus
B7
rit.
with pedal

Bdim/F
C#7
F#m7♭5
Am/E
B/D#
B7
Em7♭5
Gm/D
A/C#
A7
Dm7♭5
Fm/C
G/B
G#dim7
A
Tempo I
A5
When I was young, I nev-er
Dm6/A
A
Em6/G
F#7sus
F#7
need - ed an - y - one,
and mak-ing love was just for fun.
Bm
Dm
A/C#
Bm7♭5
Bm7♭5/E
A
Those days are gone.
All by my - self,
molto rit.
a tempo

C♯m7
4fr
G6
F♯7sus
F♯7
Bm
don't wan-na be all by my - self an-y-
Bm7♭5
D♭
Fm7
more.
C♭6
B♭7sus
B♭7
E♭m
G♭m
D♭
All by my - self,
Repeat and Fade
Fm7
C♭6
B♭7sus
B♭7
E♭m
E♭dim/B♭♭
A♭7
4fr
don't wan-na live all by my - self an-y-more.

ALONE

Words and Music by BARRY GIBB,
ROBIN GIBB and MAURICE GIBB

Gsus2
G(add2)
D
was an i - ron man. I had a mas - ter plan, but I was a - lone.
make - be - lieve you care. I feel you ev - 'ry - where, but I'm still a - lone.
I could hear you breath - ing with a sigh of the wind. I re -
I'm on a wheel of for - tune with a twist of fate 'cause I
G(add2)
mem - ber how your bod - y start - ed trem - bl - ing. Oh, what a night it's been, and
know it is - n't heav - en. Is it love or hate? Am I the sub - ject of the pain? Am
D
To Coda
for the state I'm in, I'm still a - lone. And all the
I the stran - ger in the rain? I am a - lone. And is there

Bm
Em7
A
wonders made for the Earth and all the hearts in all cre-
Bm
G
D
a-tion, some-how I al-ways end up a-lone,
al-ways end up a-lone.
So, I play, (sha la) I'll wait,
Bm
Em7
(I'll wait) 'cause you know that love takes time.
We came

D
Bm
Em7
(sha la) so far, (so far) just the beat of a lone - ly heart,
F♯m
Gmaj9
and it's mine.
D
And I don't want to be a - lone.
D.S. al Coda
Well, since I

CODA
Bm
Em7
A
glo - ry there to be-hold? May-be it's my i-mag-i-
won - ders made for the Earth and all the hearts in all cre-
Bm
Em7
A
na - tion,
a - tion,
an-oth-er sto - ry there to be told. So, I play,
D
Bm
Em7
(sha la) I'll wait, (in time) and I pray it's not too late.
D
Bm
We came, (sha la) so far, (so far) just the beat

Em7
F♯m
of a lone - ly heart,
and it's mine.
Gmaj9
1
And I don't want to be a -
D
lone.
And all the
2
And I don't want to be a -

D
lone. Gone, but not out of sight. I'm
stone. Shine and search for the light, and
caught in the rain and there's no one home.
soon - er or lat - er you'll be cruis - ing on your o -
Face the heat of the night. The
cean and clean out of sight. I'm
Repeat and Fade
one that you love's got a heart that's made of
caught in the rain and there's no one home.

BARELY BREATHING

Words and Music by
DUNCAN SHEIK

D
Em7
A
You real - ly had me go - ing, wish - ing on a star. The black - holes that sur - round
C(add9)
D
you are heav - i - er by far. I be - lieved in your con - fu -
Em7
A
- sion, so com - plete - ly torn. It must have been that yes -
- ing what's it all a - bout. It used to be so cer -
C(add9)
D
- ter - day was the day that I was born. There's not much to ex - am -
- tain. Now I can't fig - ure out. What is this at - trac -

Em7
A
- ine, noth-ing left to hide. You real - ly can't be se -
- tion? Don't it fill the day, and noth - ing left to rea -
C(add9)
D
Fmaj9
- ri-ous, you have to ask me why I say good - bye.
- son, and on - ly you to blame. Will it ev-er change?
C(add9)
'Cause I am bare - ly breath - ing, and I can't find
G(add9)
Am7
the air. Don't know who I'm kid - ding, i - mag - in - ing you

Fmaj9
C(add9)
G(add9)
care. And I could stand here wait - ing, ooh, for an-oth-er day. I don't sup-pose it's worth
Am7
Fmaj9
the price, it's worth the price, the price that I would pay.
1
And ev - 'ry - one keeps ask -
2, 3
C(add9)
G(add9)
Am7
But I'm think-ing it o - ver an - y - way.
3
3

Fmaj9
C(add9)
G(add9)
I'm think-ing it o - ver an - y-way.
Am7
Fmaj7
To Coda
Oh.
D
I come to find
Am9
Cmaj9
Gm9
I may nev-er know.
A chang - ing mind,
is it friend or foe?

D
Am9
Cmaj9
I rise _ a - bove, _
I sink be - low, ____
and ev - 'ry time _
Gm9
you come _ and go. ___
Please _ don't
come _ and go. ______
Fmaj7
D.S. al Coda
'Cause I _ am bare - ly breath -
CODA
Fmaj9
And I know what you're do -
- ing.
I see it all ________ too clear.
rit.

BUTTERFLY KISSES

Words and Music by RANDY THOMAS
and BOB CARLISLE

Dm7
C/E
F
Gsus
3 fr
G
she talks to Je - sus, and I close my eyes, and I
per - fume and make - up from rib - ons and curls,
asked me what I'm think - ing, and I said, "I'm not sure. I just
F/A
G/B
C
F
thank God for all of the joy in my life.
try - ing her wings out in a great big world.
feel like I'm los - ing my ba - by girl."
G7sus
Csus(add2)
C
Oh, but most of all, for but - ter - fly kiss - es af - ter
But I re - mem - ber but - ter - fly kiss - es af - ter
Then she leaned o - ver, gave me but - ter - fly kiss - es with her

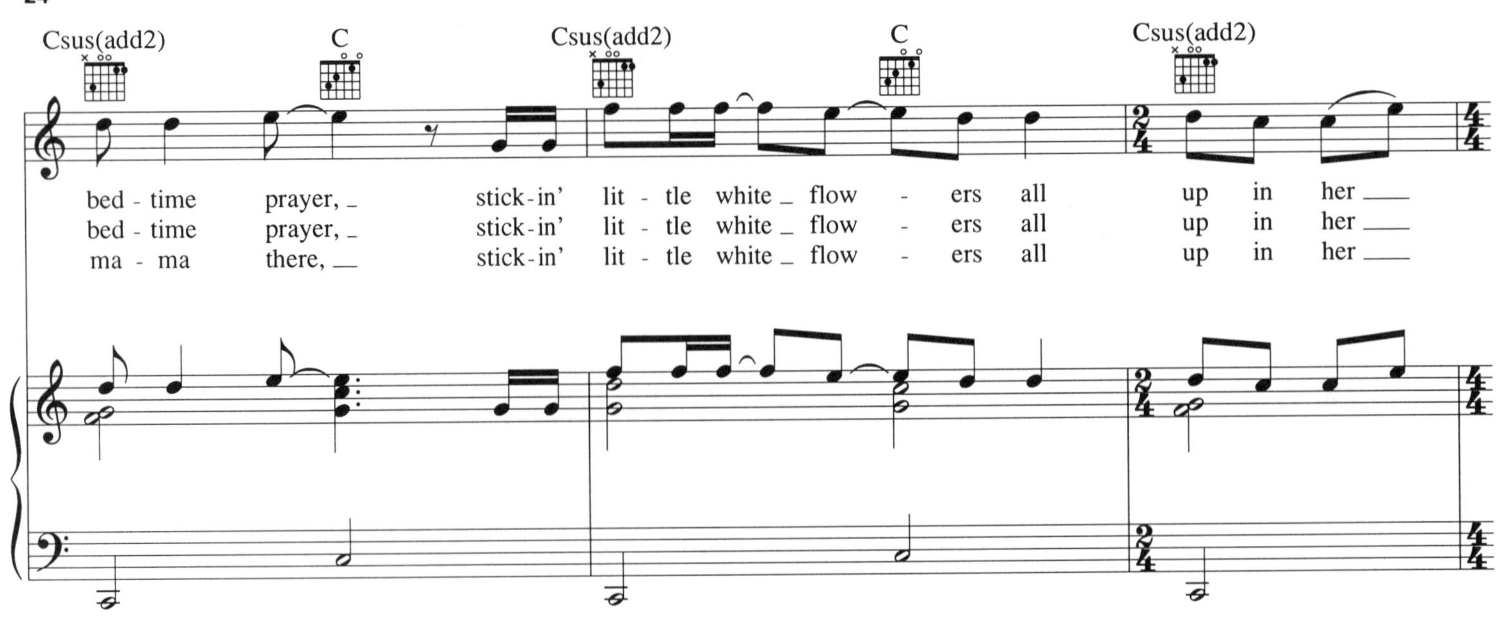
Csus(add2)
C
Csus(add2)
C
Csus(add2)
bed - time prayer, _ stick-in' lit - tle white _ flow - ers all up in her ___
bed - time prayer, _ stick-in' lit - tle white _ flow - ers all up in her ___
ma - ma there, __ stick-in' lit - tle white _ flow - ers all up in her ___

Am
G
F
hair. "Walk be - side __ the po - ny, dad - dy, it's
hair. "You know how much _ I love __ you, dad - dy, but if
hair. "Walk me down _ the aisle, _ dad - dy, it's

C/E
F
my first ride. ___ I know the cake _ looks fun - ny, dad - dy, but
you don't mind, ___ I'm on - ly goin' _ to kiss __ you on ___ the
just a - bout time. Does my wed - ding gown _ look pret - ty, dad - dy? Dad -

C/E
F/A
G/B
I sure tried." ___
cheek this time." ___
dy, don't cry." ___
Oh, with all that I've ___ done wrong, ___ I must have done
C
D7sus
D7
some - thing right ___
to de - serve
a
her
her
rit.
To Coda
F
G5
3fr
Csus(add2)
C
hug
love
love
ev-'ry morn - ing and but-ter-fly kiss-es ___ at night. ___
a tempo
1
Csus(add2)
C
Csus(add2)
C
G/A
F/G
C(add2)

2
Csus(add2)
C
E♭
3 fr
G7sus/D
(All the pre - cious time.)
Like the
Csus(add2)
C
Csus(add2)
C
wind, the years go by.
(Pre - cious but - ter -
E♭
3 fr
G7sus/D
F/A
Dm7
G7
D.S. al Coda
fly,
spread your wings and fly.)
CODA
G7sus
F/A
but - ter - fly kiss - es.
I could - n't ask God for more.
Man,

G/B
Ab maj7
this is what love is. I know I've got-ta let her go, but I'll
C/G
F
al - ways re-mem - ber ev - 'ry hug in the morn - ing and
molto rit.
a tempo
G7sus
Csus(add2)
C
Csus(add2)
C
but-ter-fly kiss-es.
Csus(add2)
C
G/A
F/G
C
molto rit.

CANDLE IN THE WIND 1997

In loving memory of Diana, Princess of Wales

Music by ELTON JOHN
Words by BERNIE TAUPIN

E7
A
and you whis-pered to those in pain. Now you be-long to
the truth brings us to tears. All our words can-
E/G#
A
Asus
heav-en, and the stars spell out your name.
not ex-press the joy you've brought us through the years.
A
B
E
And it seems to me you lived your life like a can-dle in the wind,
A
E
B
nev-er fad-ing with the sun - set when the rain set in.

Bsus
2fr
B
A
And your foot-steps will al-ways fall here a-long
C♯m
4fr
To Coda
B
Eng-land's green-est hills. Your can-dle's burned out long be-fore
3
Bsus
2fr
B
A
E/G♯
F♯m7
your leg-end ev-er will.
E
B
E/B
B

A
E/G♯
F♯m7
E
B
B7
E
E7/G♯
A
Good-bye, Eng-land's rose; may you ev-er grow in our hearts.
E/G♯
You were the grace that placed it-self where lives were torn a-part.
A
Asus
A
E
Good-bye, Eng-land's rose,

E7/G♯
A
from a coun - try lost with - out your soul, who'll miss the wings of your com -
E/G♯
A
Asus
pas - sion more than you will ev - er know.
A
D.S. al Coda
And it
CODA
B
can - dle's burned out long be - fore
E/B
B
A
E/G♯
F♯m7
E
your leg - end ev - er will.
rit.

THE FRESHMEN

Words and Music by
BRIAN VANDER ARK

E(add9)
A5
5 fr
C♯m
4 fr
guilt strick-en, sob-bin' with my head on the floor. Stop 'em, ba - by's breath, and a
guilt strick-en, sob-bin' with his head on the floor. Thinks a - bout her now and how he
guilt strick-en, sob-bin' with our heads on the floor. We fell through the ice when we
A
C♯m
B
A
shoe - ful of rice, no,
nev - er real - ly wept. He says
tried not to slip. We'd say
can't be held re - spon - si - ble,
C♯m
B
A
C♯m
B
'cause she was touch - ing her face.
I
A
C♯m
B
A
To Coda
won't be held re - spon - si - ble.
She fell in love in the first place.

E(add9)
A
C♯m
4fr
For the life of me, I can - not re - mem - ber what made us think that we were
A
E(add9)
A
wise and we'd nev - er com - pro - mise. For the life of me, I can - not be - lieve we'd
C♯m
4fr
A
1
E(add9)
ev - er die for these sins. We were mere - ly fresh - men.
A
C♯m(add9)
2fr
A
My best

2
E/G♯
A
E
B
E/G♯
A
Hey, yeah, yeah, yeah, yeah.
E
B
E/G♯
A
E
B
Hey, yeah.
Hey, yeah,
E/G♯
A
E
B(add4)
D.S. al Coda
yeah, yeah, yeah.
3
3
CODA
E(add9)
A
C♯m
4fr
B
For the life of me, I can - not re-mem-ber what made us think that we were

A
E(add9)
A
wise and we'd nev - er com - pro - mise. For the life of me, I can - not be - lieve we'd
C♯m
4 fr
B
A
E(add9)
ev - er die for these sins. We were mere - ly fresh - men. We
A
C♯m(add9)
2 fr
A
were mere - ly fresh - men. We were on - ly fresh - men.
E(add9)
A
C♯m(add9)
2 fr
A5
5 fr

DON'T CRY FOR ME ARGENTINA

from EVITA

Words by TIM RICE
Music by ANDREW LLOYD WEBBER

A Tempo
B
E/B
Eva: It won't be eas - y, you'll think it strange when I
F♯7/B
3
try to ex - plain how I feel, that I still need your love af - ter
B
G♯m/B
all that I've done. You won't be - lieve me.
C♯
C♯/B
3
3
All you will see is a girl you once knew, al - though she's dressed up to the

F♯/A♯
C♯7
F♯
nines at six - es and sev - ens with you.
B
E/B
I had to let it hap-pen, I had to change; could-n't stay all my life down at
F♯7/B
B
heel, look-ing out of the win-dow, stay-ing out of the sun. So I chose
G♯m/B
C♯7
free - dom, run - ning a - round try - ing ev - 'ry - thing new, but

C♯/B
F♯/A♯
C♯7
noth - ing im - pressed me at all. I nev - er ex - pect - ed it
Slow Tango feel
F♯
B
to. Don't cry for me, Ar - gen - ti - na, the
E/B
B
F♯
truth is I nev - er left you. All through my wild days, my mad ex -
G♯m
4fr
Bmaj7
Emaj7
ist - ence, I kept my prom - ise. Don't keep your dis - tance

B
And as for for - tune and as for
E/B
F#/B
fame, I nev - er in - vit - ed them in, though it
F#7
B
3
seemed to the world they were all I de - sired. They are il -
G#m/B
C#7
lu - sions, they're not the so - lu - tions they prom - ised to be. The

C♯/B
F♯/A♯
C♯7
an - swer was here all the time.
I love you and hope you love
F♯
Slower
B
me.
Don't cry for me, Ar - gen - ti - na.
(humming): Mmm
rall.
E
B
F♯
G♯m
4 fr
Bmaj7

B
E/B
B
Don't cry for me, Ar - gen - ti - na, the truth is I nev - er
F♯
G♯m
4fr
left you. All through my wild days, my mad ex - ist - ence, I kept my
Bmaj7
Emaj7
prom - ise. Don't keep your dis - tance. Have I said too much? There's
D♯m7
noth-ing more I can think of to say to you. But

Emaj7
B
all you have to do is look at me to know that ev - 'ry word is true.
rit.
Grandioso
B
E/B
B
F♯
G♯m
4fr
ten. ten. ten.
ten. ten. ten.
Bmaj7
Emaj7
B
poco rit.

EVERYTIME I CLOSE MY EYES

Words and Music by
BABYFACE

Gm7
3 fr
B♭/C
Am/C
C/B♭
Am7
Am7/D
A♭13♭5
win-ter. It feels like Christ - mas in June. It feels like heav - en has o -
won-der the sun al-ways shines when I'm near you. It's just a bless - ing that I
Gm7
3 fr
Am7
B♭/C
F
Am/E
- pened up its gates for me and you.
have found some-bod - y like you.
And ev - 'ry - time I close my eyes, I
Dm
F/C
B♭maj9
B♭/C
thank the Lord that I've got you and you've got me, too. And
F
Am/E
Dm
F/C
B♭maj9
To Coda
ev - 'ry - time I think of it, I pinch my - self 'cause I don't be - lieve it's true that

C7sus
F
B♭maj9
B♭6
F
some-one like you loves me too.
D♭maj9
Gm7/C
Gm7/C
C7
Dm
some-one like you loves me too. To
A7/C♯
F/C
G7/B
think of all the nights I've cried my-self to sleep.
You real-ly ought-a know how much you mean to me.
Gm7
C/F
F/E♭
B♭/C
It's on-ly right that you be in my life right here with me. Oh, ba-by, ba-by,

F
Am7/E
Dm
Fmaj7/C
B♭maj9
1
B♭maj7/C
6fr
C7
yeah.
Sax solo ad lib.
2
B♭maj7
C7
D.S. al Coda
And
CODA
Gm7(add4)
3fr
some - one like you
C7sus
F
B♭maj9
B♭6
F
loves me too,
D♭maj9
3fr
Gm7/C
F
loves me too.

FLY LIKE AN EAGLE

featured in the Motion Picture SPACE JAM

Words and Music by
STEVE MILLER

D/A
Am9
- ture.
Time keeps on slip-pin', slip-pin',
D/A
Am9
slip-pin' in - to the fu - ture.
D/A
Am
D/A
Said I wan-na fly like an ea - gle
Dm/A
Am
D/A
to the sea, fly like an ea - gle. Let the

Dm/A
Am
D/A
spir - it car - ry me. I wan - na fly,
fly right in - to the fu -
To Coda
Am9
- ture. I wan - na feed the ba - bies who
can't get e - nough to eat. Wan - na shoe the chil - dren with no

D/A
Am9
shoes on their feet. I wan-na house the peo - ple
liv-in' in the street. Oh yeah, there's a so-lu - tion. Just let me fly
D.S. al Coda
CODA
Dm/A
Am
N.C.
- ture. Time keeps on slip-pin', slip-pin',
Am7
slip-pin' in - to the fu - ture.

Am
N.C.
Time flies, don't it, babe? _ Do do do do.
Am
N.C.
Do do do do. Do do do do. Do do do do.
Am D/A Dm/A Am D/A
1
Dm/A Am
2
Dm/A Am
I wan - na fly _

Am
D/A
Dm/A
Am
like an ea - gle
to the sea,
fly
Lead vocal ad lib.
D/A
Dm/A
Am
like an ea - gle. Let my spir - it car - ry me. I wan - na
D/A
Dm/A
Am
fly,
D/A
Dm/A
Am
Repeat and Fade
fly right in - to the fu - ture. Let me fly

GO THE DISTANCE

from Walt Disney Pictures' HERCULES

Music by ALAN MENKEN
Lyrics by DAVID ZIPPEL

G A Bm G F♯ Bm D/A G Asus A
see my face, and a voice keeps say-ing this is where I'm meant to be. I'll be
worth the wait. It might take a life-time, but some-how I'll see it through. And I
D(add9)/F♯ Em/G D/A A A/G D(add9)/F♯ Em/G
there some-day. I can go the dis-tance. I will find my way
won't look back. I can go the dis-tance. And I'll stay on track. No, I
D/A A A/G D(add9)/F♯ G
1 Bm7
2fr
if I can be strong. I know ev-'ry mile will be worth my while.
won't ac-cept de-feat. It's an up-hill slope, but I
Em7 G A D A/C♯ Bm D/A Gmaj7 G/A
When I go the dis-tance, I'll be right where I be-

2
D A/D G/D D A/D G/D Bm7 Em7
2fr
long. Down an won't lose hope till I
G A D A/C♯ Bm D/A G Asus A D A/D G/D
go the dis-tance and my jour - ney is com - plete. Oh,
D A/D G/D F B♭/D C/E A/C♯
yeah. But to look be-yond the glo - ry is the hard - est part, for a
D G F♯/A♯ E/G♯ F♯/A♯ B
he-ro's strength is meas - ured by his heart.

E/G♯ F♯/A♯ B G/B A/C♯ D Bm Em7♭5/B♭
D/A G/A A7
Like a
rall.
D(add9)/F♯ Em/G D/A A G D(add9)/F♯ Em/G
shoot - ing star, I will go the dis - tance. I will search the world.
a tempo
D/A A G D(add9)/F♯ E/G♯ F♯/A♯ Bm
I will face its harms. I don't care how far. I can go the dis - tance till I

G A D A/C# Bm D/A G Asus A
find my he - ro's wel - come wait - ing in your
rit.
Broadly
D5
Asus
arms. I will
D(add9)/F# Gmaj7 Bm7 Em11
search the world. I will face its harms till I
G A D A/C# Bm D/A G A7sus G/B A/C# D
find my he - ro's wel - come wait - ing in your arms.
rit.

I SAY A LITTLE PRAYER

featured in the Tri-Star Motion Picture MY BEST FRIEND'S WEDDING

Lyric by HAL DAVID
Music by BURT BACHARACH

F♯m7
B
say a lit - tle prayer for you.
say a lit - tle prayer for you.
say a lit - tle prayer for you.)
Em7
Am7
While comb - ing my hair now, and won - d'ring what
At work, I just take time, and all through my
D
Gmaj7
F♯m7
dress to wear now,
cof - fee break time,
I say a lit - tle prayer for you.
End solo
B
C
D/C
For - ev - er, for - ev - er, you'll

Bm7
G/B
F/G
G
C
D/C
2fr
stay in my heart and I will love you. For - ev - er and ev - er, we
nev - er will part. Oh, how I'll love you. To - geth - er, to - geth - er, that's
how it must be. To live with - out you would on - ly mean heart - break for
3
B
To Coda
1
2
D.S. al Coda
me.

CODA
Em7
Am7
My dar - ling, be - lieve me,
C/D
for me there is no one but
Gmaj7
Am7/D
Gmaj7
you. Please love me, too.
Am7/D
Gmaj7
Am7/D
I'm in love with you, an - swer my

Gmaj7
Am7/D
Gmaj7
prayer.
Say you love me, too.
Am7/D
Gmaj7
Why don't you an - swer my prayer?
Am7/D
Repeat and Fade
You know, ev - 'ry day I say a lit - tle

HARD TO SAY I'M SORRY

Words and Music by PETER CETERA
and DAVID FOSTER

B♭/A♭
E♭
3fr
E - ven lov - ers need a hol - i - day,
Would - n't wan - na be swept a - way,
Gm7
3fr
A♭
4fr
far a - way from each
far a - way from the
E♭/B♭
6fr
B♭7
Cm7
3fr
Fm7
oth - er.
one that I love.
Hold me now.
It's
B♭sus
E♭
3fr
E♭/D
3fr
Cm7
3fr
hard for me to say, "I'm sor - ry."
I just

To Coda
Fm7
B♭
want you to stay.
know,
rall.
E♭
A♭sus2/C
B♭/D
And af - ter all that you've been through,
a tempo
G/B
Cm
F/A
I will make it up to you. I prom -
Fm7
B♭
E♭
- ise you, ba - by. And af - ter

A♭sus2/C
B♭/D
G/B
all that's been said and done, you're just
Cm
F/A
B♭sus
a part of me I can't let go.
B♭
B♭(sus2/4)
B♭
D.S. al Coda
CODA
B♭sus
B♭
Cm7
you to know. Hold me now.

Fm7
B♭sus
B♭
E♭
3 fr
I real - ly wan - na tell you I'm sor - ry.
Cm7
3 fr
Fm7
B♭sus
B♭/A♭
B♭
I could nev - er let you go, ah.
G♭
C♭sus2/E♭
4 fr
D♭/F
Af - ter all that we've been through,
B♭/D
E♭m
A♭7/C
2 fr
D♭sus
4 fr
D♭
I will make it up to you, I prom - ise to.

Ebm7
Db/F
Gb
Cbsus2/Eb
Db/F
And af - ter all that's been said and done,
Bb/D
Ebm
Ab/C
Abm6/9/Cb
you're just a part of me I can't let
Bbsus
Bb
go.
Eb
I can't let go.
rit.

I BELIEVE IN YOU AND ME

from the Touchstone Motion Picture THE PREACHER'S WIFE

Words and Music by DAVID WOLFERT
and SANDY LINZER

Em7
Dm7
G7sus
me, oh, yes, you will. And I be-lieve in dreams
C
C/B♭
a-gain. I be-lieve that love will nev-er end. And
Fmaj7/A
Fm7
B♭9
C9/G
like the riv-er finds the sea, I was lost, now I'm
Em7
Am7
Dm7
F/G
C
F/G
free 'cause I be-lieve in you and me. I will nev-er leave

C
C/B♭
your side. I will nev - er hurt your pride. When all the
Fmaj7
A♭/B♭
chips are down, babe, then I will al-ways be a - round.
C
G/A
Am7
Em7
Just to be right where you are, my love. You know I love
Dm7
F/G
C
you, boy. I'll nev-er leave you out. I will al-ways

C/B♭
Fmaj7/A
let you in, boy, oh, ba-by, to pla-ces no one's ev - er been.
A♭/B♭
B♭7
C/G
Em7
Am7
Deep in-side, can't you see that
Dm7
F/G
C
Em7
Am7
I be-lieve in you and me.
May-be I'm a fool to
Em7
Am7
Dm
Dm♯7
Dm7
feel the way I do.
I would play the fool for-ev-er

G7sus
Ab7sus
just to be with you for-ev-er. I be-lieve in
Db
Db/B
mir-a-cles, and love's a mir-a-cle, and yes,
Gbmaj7
A/B
Db/B F#m6/A Db/Gb
ba-by, you're my dream come true. I, I was
Db/Ab
4fr
Fm7
Bbm7
lost, now I'm free, oh ba-by, 'cause

Ebm7
Absus2
Cb/Db
Db7
I be - lieve, I do be-lieve in you and me. See, I'm
Gbmaj7
Fm7
Bbm7
lost, now I'm free 'cause
Ebm7
Gb/Ab
N.C.
Db(add2)
I be-lieve in you and me.
L.H.
Db/Cb
Gbmaj7
Ebm7
Gb/Ab
Db(add9)

IT'S ALL COMING BACK TO ME NOW

Words and Music by
JIM STEINMAN

Dm Em Am Dm F
tears turned to dust, and I just knew my eyes were dry - ing out for - ev - er.
C/G G Em Am F G7 C
I fin - ished cry - ing in the in - stant that you left, and I
Thought you were his - t'ry with the slam - ming of the door, and I
Em7 Am F Gsus G Em7 Am
3 fr
can't re - mem - ber where or when or how. And I ban - ished ev - 'ry mem - 'ry you and I
made my - self so strong a - gain some - how. And I nev - er wast - ed an - y of my time
F G F F/G
had ev - er made. But when you
on you since then. But if I
rit.
a tempo

C
G/B
touch me like this, and you hold me like that, I just
touch you like this, and if you kiss me like that, it was
Am7
Dm7
F
G7
have to ad - mit that it's all com - ing back to me. When I
so long a - go, but it's all com - ing back to me. If you
C
G/B
touch you like this, and I hold you like that, it's so
touch me like this, and if I kiss you like that, it was
Am7
Dm7
E
F
G7
hard to be - lieve, but it's all com - ing back to me.
gone with the wind, but it's all com - ing back to me.
(It's

C
F
G
all com - ing back, it's all com - ing back to me now.) There were
Am7
F
Em7
F
mo - ments of gold, and there were flash - es of light. There were
Am7
F
Em7
F
things I'd we'd nev - er do a - gain, but then they'd al - ways seemed right. There were
Am7
Em7
Am7
F
Dm7
nights of end-less pleas-ure. It was more than a - ny all your lov - ers in love.

F/G
C
Ba - by, ba - by if I kiss you like this, and if you
Ba - by, ba - by, ba - by, when you touch me like this, and when you
rall.
a tempo
G/B
Am7
Dm7
whis - per like that, it was lost long a - go, but it's all
hold me like that, it was gone with the wind, but it's all
F
G7
C
com - ing back to me. If you want me like this, and if you
com - ing back to me. When you see me like this, and when I
G/B
Am7
Dm7
need me like that, it was that long a - go, but it's all
see you like that, then we've seen what we want to see, all

F
G7
Am7
Dm7
coming back to me. It's so hard to resist, and it's all
coming back to me. The flesh and the fantasies all
F
G7
Am7
Dm7
F
coming back to me.
coming back to me.
I can barely recall, but it's all
G
To Coda
Am
G/B
coming back to me now.
3
3
F
Dm7
D.S. al Coda
CODA
Am
G

Bm7
2 fr
G/B
C
-bles that I have to face.
Oh, but I won't let my spir-it fail
me. Mm, I won't let
Bm7/E
my spir-it go
Em
un-til I get
C
to my des-ti-na-tion.
Em7
I'm gon-na take it slow
D7sus
be-cause I'm mak-ing it up
G
step by step. You know I'm tak-

D/F♯
Em7
ing it bit by bit, bit by bit, come on, stone by stone,
Bm7
2fr
Gmaj7/B
yeah, brick by brick.
Brick by brick by brick by brick.
C
Cmaj7
Bm7/E
Mm. Step by step, step by step, oh, day by day,
Cmaj7
mile by mile, ooh.

Em7
D7sus
To Coda
G
Go your own way, go your own way. Don't give up.
D/F#
You've got to hold on to what you've got. Oh, ba -
Em7
Bm7
2fr
by, don't give up. You've got to keep on mov - in', don't
Cmaj7
stop. Yeah, yeah. I know you're hurt - ing,

Em9
Cmaj7
and I know you're blue.
I know you're hurt-
Em7
D7sus
- ing, but don't let the bad things get to you.
N.C.
G
D.S. al Coda
CODA
G
I'm tak-ing it step by step.
Come on, babe, got to keep mov-ing.
D/F#
Come on, babe, got to keep mov-ing. Come on, babe, got to keep mov-in'. Come on, babe, got to keep mov-in'.
(Bit by bit.)

Em7
Bm7
2 fr
Come on, babe, got _ to keep mov-in'. Come on, babe, got _ to keep mov-in.' Come on, babe, got _ to keep mov-in.'
(Stone by stone.) _ (Yeah.) _ (Brick by brick.)
Cmaj7
Come on, ba - by. Come on, babe, got _ to keep mov-in'. Come on, babe, got _ to keep mov-in'.
(Step by step.)
Bm7/E
Em
Cmaj7
Come on, babe, got _ to keep mov-in'. Come on, babe, got _ to keep mov - in'. Come on, babe, got _ to keep mov-in'.
(Day by day.) (Mile by mile.) _
Bm7/E
D7sus
Repeat and Fade
Come on, babe, got _ to keep mov-in'. Come on, babe, got _ to keep mov-in'. Come on, babe, got _ to keep mov-in'.
(Go your own way.) (Go your own way.) _

WANNABE

Words and Music by MATT ROWE,
RICHARD STANNARD and SPICE GIRLS

B D E A A♯
I wan-na, I wan-na, I wan-na, I wan-na real-ly real-ly real-ly wan-na zig-a-zig ha.
F♯ G♯m E B F♯ G♯m
fr4
1. If you want my fu-ture, for-get my past. If you wan-na get with me,
(Verse 2 see block lyric)
E B F♯ G♯m E B
bet-ter make it fast. Now don't go wast-ing my pre-cious time,
F♯ G♯m E B
get your act to-ge-ther, we could be just fine. I'll

B
D
tell you what I want, what I real - ly real - ly want, so
E
A
A♯
tell me what you want, what you real - ly real - ly want. I wan - na,
B
D
E
A
A♯
I wan-na, I wan-na, I wan-na, I wan-na real-ly real-ly real-ly wan-na zig - a - zig ha.
F♯
G♯m
fr4
E
B
If you wan-na be my lov - er, you got - ta get with my friends.

F♯
G♯m
fr4
E
B
Make it last for - ev - er, friend - ship nev - er ends.
If you wan - na be my lov - er, you have got to give,
1, 3.
To Coda
tak - ing is too ea - sy, but that's the way it is.
2.
D
(2° vocal ad lib.)
the way it is
So here's the sto - ry from A to Z you wan - na

Verse 2:
What do you think about that now you know how I feel
Say you can handle my love, are you for real?
I won't be hasty, I'll give you a try
If you really bug me then I'll say goodbye.

YOU WERE MEANT FOR ME

Words and Music by JEWEL KILCHER
and STEVE POLTZ

G/B
C
D
pan-cakes, too. I got my ma-ple syr - up, ev-'ry-thing but you.
more bad news. My heart's be - ing bro - ken by peo - ple be - ing used.
turn the sheets down and then I take a deep breath, a good look a - round.
3
C(add9)
G/B
C
I break the yolks and make a smil - ey face. I kind - a like it in my
Put on my coat in the pour - ing rain. I saw a mov - ie, it just
Put on my p j's and hop in - to bed. I'm half a - live, but I feel
Em
C(add9)
G/B
brand new place. Wipe the spots up o - ver me, don't leave my keys in the door. I
was - n't the same 'cause it was hap - py or I was sad, and
most - ly dead. I try and tell my - self it'll be all right.

C
D
C
nev - er put wet towels on the floor an - y - more
it made me miss you, oh, so bad 'cause dreams last
I just should-n't think an - y - more to - night
D
G
D/F#
Em7
Em7/D
so long e - ven af - ter you're gone.
C
D
G
D/F#
I know that you love me, and soon you will see
Em
Em/D
C
D
To Coda
you were meant for me and I was meant for

Em
1
2
you.
I
Am7
D
Bm
D
go a-bout my bus - 'ness. I'm do-ing fine. Be-sides, what would I say if I had
C
G/D
Am7
D
you on the line? Same old sto-ry, not much to say.
Freely
Bm7
2fr
Em
Tempo Primo
C(add9)
Hearts are bro-ken ev-'ry-day.

G/B
C
1
Em
2
Em
D.S. al Coda
CODA
Em
you.
Yeah, _
you were
C
D
C(add9)
meant for me,
and
I
was meant for
you.
G/B
C
Em
rit.

WHERE HAVE ALL THE COWBOYS GONE?

Words and Music by
PAULA COLE

N.C.
N.C.
Oh, you get me read - y in your fif - ty - six Chev - y. Why don't we go sit down in the shade? Take
don't you stay the eve - ning, kick back and watch the T V, and I'll fix a lit - tle some - thing to eat. Oh,
fi - n'lly sold the Chev - y when we had an - oth - er ba - by and you took that job in Ten - nes - see. You
shel - ter on my front porch, the dan - de - li - on sun scorch and
I know your back hurts from work - in' on the trac - tor. How
made friends at the farm and you join 'em at the bar al - most

Gmaj7
like a glass of cold lem-on-ade?
do you take your cof - fee, my sweet?
ev - 'ry sin - gle day of the week.
I will do the laun - dry
I will raise the chil - dren
I will wash the dish - es
A
Bm
C♯m
4fr
if you pay all the bills.
if you pay all the bills.
while you go have a beer.
F♯m
C♯m
F♯m
Where is my John Wayne?
Where is my
C♯m
F♯m
C♯m
prai - rie sun?
Where is my hap - py end - ing?

D(add2)
To Coda
E(add2)
Bm7
2 fr
Where have all the cow - boys gone?
C#m
4 fr
D(add2)
1
E(add2)
Why
2
E(add2)
Gmaj7
I am wear - ing my new dress
to-night, but you don't, but you don't e - ven no - tice
Bm

C♯m
4fr
D(add2)
E(add2)
me.
Say our good -
Bm7
2fr
C♯m
4fr
D(add2)
- byes,
say our good - byes,
say our good - byes.
E(add2)
N.C.
D.S. al Coda
Spoken: We
CODA
E(add2)
F♯m
- boys gone?
Where is my

C#m
4fr
F#m
C#m
4fr
Marl - bor - o Man?
Where is his shin - y gun?
F#m
C#m
4fr
D(add2)
Where is my lone - ly ran - ger?
Where have all the cow -
E(add2)
Bm7
2fr
C#m
4fr
Repeat ad lib.
- boys gone?
D(add2)
E

Contemporary Classics

Your favorite songs for piano, voice and guitar.

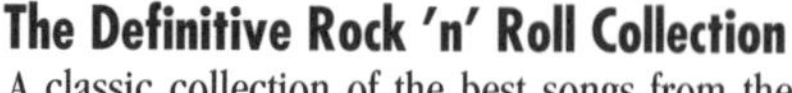

The Definitive Rock 'n' Roll Collection

A classic collection of the best songs from the early rock 'n' roll years – 1955-1966. 97 songs, including: Barbara Ann • Chantilly Lace • Dream Lover • Duke Of Earl • Earth Angel • Great Balls Of Fire • Louie, Louie • Rock Around The Clock • Ruby Baby • Runaway • (Seven Little Girls) Sitting In The Back Seat • Stay • Surfin' U.S.A. • Wild Thing • Woolly Bully • and more.

00490195 .... $27.95

The Big Book Of Rock

78 of rock's biggest hits, including: Addicted To Love • American Pie • Born To Be Wild • Cold As Ice • Dust In The Wind • Free Bird • Goodbye Yellow Brick Road • Groovin' • Hey Jude • I Love Rock N Roll • Lay Down Sally • Layla • Livin' On A Prayer • Louie Louie • Maggie May • Me And Bobby McGee • Monday, Monday • Owner Of A Lonely Heart • Shout • Walk This Way • We Didn't Start The Fire • You Really Got Me • and more.

00311566 .... $19.95

Big Book Of Movie And TV Themes

Over 90 familiar themes, including: Alfred Hitchcock Theme • Beauty And The Beast • Candle On The Water • Theme From *E.T.* • Endless Love • Hawaii Five-O • I Love Lucy • Theme From *Jaws* • Jetsons • Major Dad Theme • The Masterpiece • Mickey Mouse March • The Munsters Theme • Theme From *Murder, She Wrote* • Mystery • Somewhere Out There • Unchained Melody • Won't You Be My Neighbor • and more!

00311582 .... $19.95

The Best Rock Songs Ever

70 of the best rock songs from yesterday and today, including: All Day And All Of The Night • All Shook Up • Ballroom Blitz • Bennie And The Jets • Blue Suede Shoes • Born To Be Wild • Boys Are Back In Town • Every Breath You Take • Faith • Free Bird • Hey Jude • I Still Haven't Found What I'm Looking For • Livin' On A Prayer • Lola • Louie Louie • Maggie May • Money • (She's) Some Kind Of Wonderful • Takin' Care Of Business • Walk This Way • We Didn't Start The Fire • We Got The Beat • Wild Thing • more!

00490424 .... $16.95

The Best Of 90s Rock

30 songs, including: Alive • I'd Do Anything For Love (But I Won't Do That) • Livin' On The Edge • Losing My Religion • Two Princes • Walking On Broken Glass • Wind Of Change • and more.

00311668 .... $14.95

35 Classic Hits

35 contemporary favorites, including: Beauty And The Beast • Dust In The Wind • Just The Way You Are • Moon River • The River Of Dreams • Somewhere Out There • Tears In Heaven • When I Fall In Love • A Whole New World (Aladdin's Theme) • and more.

00311654 .... $12.95

55 Contemporary Standards

55 favorites, including: Alfie • Beauty And The Beast • Can't Help Falling In Love • Candle In The Wind • Have I Told You Lately • How Am I Supposed To Live Without You • Memory • The River Of Dreams • Sea Of Love • Tears In Heaven • Up Where We Belong • When I Fall In Love • and more.

00311670 .... $15.95

Women of Modern Rock

25 songs from contemporary chanteuses, including: As I Lay Me Down • Connection • Feed The Tree • Galileo • Here And Now • Look What Love Has Done • Love Sneakin' Up On You • Walking On Broken Glass • You Oughta Know • Zombie • and more.

00310093 .... $14.95

Jock Rock Hits

32 stadium-shaking favorites, including: Another One Bites The Dust • The Boys Are Back In Town • Freeze-Frame • Gonna Make You Sweat (Everybody Dance Now) • I Got You (I Feel Good) • Na Na Hey Hey Kiss Him Goodbye • Rock & Roll – Part II (The Hey Song) • Shout • Tequila • We Are The Champions • We Will Rock You • Whoomp! (There It Is) • Wild Thing • and more.

00310105 .... $14.95

Rock Ballads

31 sentimental favorites, including: All For Love • Bed Of Roses • Dust In The Wind • Everybody Hurts • Right Here Waiting • Tears In Heaven • and more.

00311673 .... $14.95

FOR MORE INFORMATION, SEE YOUR LOCAL MUSIC DEALER,
OR WRITE TO:

7777 W. BLUEMOUND RD. P.O. BOX 13819 MILWAUKEE, WI 53213

Visit Hal Leonard Online at www.halleonard.com

Prices, contents & availability subject to change without notice.

0997

BIG BOOKS OF MUSIC

Our "Big Books" feature big selections of popular titles under one cover, perfect for performing musicians, holiday sing-alongs, and music aficionados. All books are arranged for piano, voice, and guitar, and feature stay-open binding, so the books lie flat without breaking the spine.

BIG BOOK OF CHILDREN'S SONGS

61 songs that children know and love! The P/V/G edition features a categorical listing of songs and ideas for musical and educational activities. Includes: The Alphabet Song • Happy Birthday To You • I Whistle A Happy Tune • It's A Small World • London Bridge • Mickey Mouse March • Old MacDonald Had A Farm • Peter Cottontail • The Rainbow Connection • Supercalifragilisticexpialidocious • This Land Is Your Land • and more!

00359261.....$12.95

GREAT BIG BOOK OF CHILDREN'S SONGS

74 classics for kids, including: ABC-DEF-GHI • Beauty And The Beast • Bein' Green • The Brady Bunch • "C" Is For Cookie • The Candy Man • Casper The Friendly Ghost • Everything Is Beautiful • I'm Popeye The Sailor Man • Kum Ba Yah • Let's Go Fly A Kite • The Marvelous Toy • Puff The Magic Dragon • Rubber Duckie • A Spoonful Of Sugar • Take Me Out To The Ballgame • Under The Sea • Won't You Be My Neighbor? • and more.

00310002.....$14.95

BIG BOOK OF CONTEMPORARY CHRISTIAN FAVORITES

A comprehensive collection of 50 songs, including: Angels • El Shaddai • Friends • The Great Adventure • I Will Be Here • Love In Any Language • Love Will Be Our Home • O Magnify The Lord • People Need The Lord • Say The Name • Turn Up The Radio • Via Dolorosa • Whatever You Ask • Where There Is Faith • and more.

00310021.....$19.95

BIG BOOK OF COUNTRY MUSIC

Includes over 60 classic and contemporary country hits: Ain't Going Down ('Til the Sun Comes Up) • Before You Kill Us All • Blue • The Greatest Man I Never Knew • I Can Love You Like That • I've Come to Expect It From You • The Keeper of the Stars • No One Else on Earth • On the Other Hand • One Boy, One Girl • Ring on Her Finger, Time on Her Hands • She's Not the Cheatin' Kind • When You Say Nothing at All • Wild Angels • more.

00310188.....$19.95

THE BIG BOOK OF BROADWAY

Songs from over 50 shows, including *Annie Get Your Gun, Carousel, Company, Guys And Dolls, Les Miserables, South Pacific, Sunset Boulevard,* and more. 76 classics, including: All I Ask Of You • Bali Ha'i • Bring Him Home • Camelot • Don't Cry For Me Argentina • Hello, Young Lovers • I Dreamed A Dream • The Impossible Dream • Mame • Memory • Oklahoma • One • People • Tomorrow • Unusual Way • and more.

00311658.....$19.95

BIG BOOK OF LATIN AMERICAN SONGS

90 favorites in their original languages, including: Amapola • Andalucia • The Breeze And I • Cherry Pink & Apple Blossom White • Desafinado • Don't Cry For Me Argentina • Flamingo • The Girl From Ipanema • How Insensitive • Kiss Of Fire • La Cucaracha • La Paloma • Little Boat • Malaguena • Meditation • Miami Beach Rumba • One Note Samba • Poinciana • Que Sera Sera • Quiet Nights Of Quiet Stars • Samba De Orfeu • So Nice (Summer Samba) • South Of The Border • Tango Of Roses • Yellow Days • Vaya Con Dios • and more!

00311562.....$19.95

THE BIG BOOK OF NOSTALGIA

More than 160 of the best songs ever written, complete with a brief history of each song, including: After The Ball • After You've Gone • Anchors Aweigh • Ballin' The Jack • Beale Street Blues • The Bells Of St. Mary's • The Entertainer • Fascination • Give My Regards To Broadway • I Ain't Got Nobody • I Wonder Who's Kissing Her Now • Let Me Call You Sweetheart • Meet Me In St. Louis, Louis • My Wild Irish Rose • Sidewalks Of New York • When Irish Eyes Are Smiling • You Made Me Love You • and more.

00310004.....$19.95

THE BIG BOOK OF STANDARDS

86 classics essential to any music library, including: April In Paris • Autumn In New York • Blue Skies • Cheek To Cheek • Heart And Soul • I Left My Heart In San Francisco • In The Mood • Isn't It Romantic? • It's Impossible • L-O-V-E • Lover, Come Back To Me • Mona Lisa • Moon River • The Nearness Of You • Out Of Nowhere • Spanish Eyes • Star Dust • Stella By Starlight • That Old Black Magic • They Say It's Wonderful • The Way We Were • What Now My Love • and more.

00311667.....$19.95

BIG BOOK OF CHRISTMAS SONGS

An outstanding collection of over 125 all-time Christmas classics, including: Angels We Have Heard On High • Auld Lang Syne • The Boar's Head Carol • Coventry Carol • Deck The Hall • The First Noel • The Friendly Beasts • God Rest Ye Merry Gentlemen • I Heard The Bells On Christmas Day • Jesu, Joy Of Man's Desiring • Joy To The World • Masters In This Hall • O Holy Night • The Story Of The Shepherd • 'Twas The Night Before Christmas • What Child Is This? • and many more.

00311520.....$19.95

BIG BOOK OF LOVE AND WEDDING SONGS

Over 80 wedding favorites, including: All I Ask Of You • Anniversary Song • Ave Maria • Could I Have This Dance • Dedicated To The One I Love • Endless Love • Forever And Ever, Amen • Here And Now • Longer • Lost In Your Eyes • So In Love • Something • Sunrise, Sunset • Through The Years • Trumpet Voluntary • The Vows Go Unbroken • You Decorated My Life • and more.

00311567.....$19.95

THE BIG BOOK OF JAZZ

75 of the world's greatest jazz classics, including: Autumn Leaves • Bewitched • Birdland • Cherokee • A Fine Romance • Flying Home • Have You Met Miss Jones • Honeysuckle Rose • How High The Moon • (I Can Recall) Spain • I've Got You Under My Skin • Jelly Roll Blues • Lullaby Of Birdland • Morning Dance • A Night In Tunisia • A Nightingale Sang In Berkeley Square • Route 66 • Take The "A" Train • and more.

00311557.....$19.95

BIG BOOK OF MOVIE AND TV THEMES

Over 90 familiar themes, including: Alfred Hitchcock Theme • Beauty And The Beast • Candle On The Water • Theme From E.T. • Endless Love • Hawaii Five-O • I Love Lucy • Theme From Jaws • Jetsons • Major Dad Theme • The Masterpiece • Mickey Mouse March • The Munsters Theme • Theme From Murder, She Wrote • Mystery • Somewhere Out There • Unchained Melody • Won't You Be My Neighbor • and more!

00311582.....$19.95

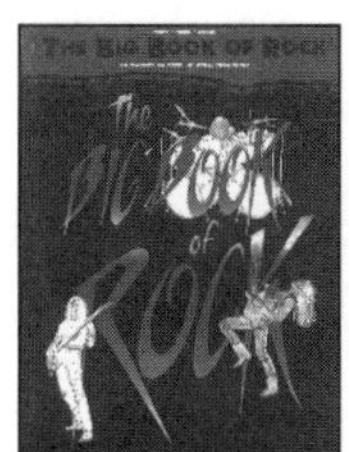

THE BIG BOOK OF ROCK

78 of rock's biggest hits, including: Addicted To Love • American Pie • Born To Be Wild • Cold As Ice • Dust In The Wind • Free Bird • Goodbye Yellow Brick Road • Groovin' • Hey Jude • I Love Rock N Roll • Lay Down Sally • Layla • Livin' On A Prayer • Louie Louie • Maggie May • Me And Bobby McGee • Monday, Monday • Owner Of A Lonely Heart • Shout • Walk This Way • We Didn't Start The Fire • You Really Got Me • and more.

00311566.....$19.95

Prices, contents, and availability subject to change without notice.

FOR MORE INFORMATION, SEE YOUR LOCAL MUSIC DEALER, OR WRITE TO:

7777 W. BLUEMOUND RD. P.O. BOX 13819 MILWAUKEE, WI 53213

0797